Waiters

Level 8 – Purple

Helpful Hints for Reading at Home

The graphemes (written letters) and phonemes (units of sound) used throughout this series are aligned with Letters and Sounds. This offers a consistent approach to learning, whether reading at home or in the classroom.

HERE IS A LIST OF PHONEMES FOR THIS PHASE OF LEARNING. AN EXAMPLE OF THE PRONUNCIATION CAN BE FOUND IN BRACKETS.

Phase 5			
ay (day)	ou (out)	ie (tie)	ea (eat)
oy (boy)	ir (girl)	ue (blue)	aw (saw)
wh (when)	ph (photo)	ew (new)	oe (toe)
au (Paul)	a_e (make)	e_e (these)	i_e (like)
o_e (home)	u_e (rule, cube)		

Phase 5 Alternative Pronunciations of Graphemes			
a (hat, what)	e (bed, she)	i (fin, find)	o (hot, so, other)
u (but, unit)	c (cat, cent)	g (got, giant)	ow (cow, blow)
ie (tied, field)	ea (eat, bread)	er (farmer, herb)	ch (chin, school, chef)
y (yes, by, very)	ou (out, shoulder, could, you)		

HERE ARE SOME WORDS WHICH YOUR CHILD MAY FIND TRICKY.

Phase 5 Tricky Words			
oh	their	people	Mr
Mrs	looked	called	asked
could			

TOP TIPS FOR HELPING YOUR CHILD TO READ:

- Allow children time to break down unfamiliar words into units of sound and then encourage children to string these sounds together to create the word.

- Encourage your child to point out any focus phonics when they are used.

- Read through the book more than once to grow confidence.

- Ask simple questions about the text to assess understanding.

- Encourage children to use illustrations as prompts.

This book focuses on /er/ and the alternative pronunciations of its grapheme. It is a Purple level 8 book band.

Can you figure out which of these people have jobs with **er** in the name?

Answers: bus driver, farmer, builder

Waiters can be the difference between a nice dinner out and an excellent dinner out. They help make mealtimes go smoothly so that people can enjoy their food without being interrupted.

Waiters are the people who help you order food when you eat out. They help with serving food after the chefs have cooked it.

When lots of people order food at the same time, it can get hectic. Waiters have to keep track of several orders at a time and make sure they do not get them mixed up.

It is important that waiters note down orders perfectly. If a customer has a food allergy, getting the order mixed up could be very bad.

©2023 **BookLife Publishing Ltd.**
King's Lynn, Norfolk, PE30 4LS, UK

ISBN 978-1-80505-092-6

All rights reserved. Printed in China.
A catalogue record for this book is available from the British Library.

Waiters
Written by Charis Mather
Designed by Isabella Croker

An Introduction to BookLife Readers...

Our Readers have been specifically created in line with the London Institute of Education's approach to book banding and are phonetically decodable and ordered to support each phase of the Letters and Sounds document.

Each book has been created to provide the best possible reading and learning experience. Our aim is to share our love of books with children, providing both emerging readers and prolific page-turners with beautiful books that are guaranteed to provoke interest and learning, regardless of ability.

BOOK BAND GRADED using the Institute of Education's approach to levelling.

PHONETICALLY DECODABLE supporting each phase of Letters and Sounds.

EXERCISES AND QUESTIONS to offer reinforcement and to ascertain comprehension.

CLEAR DESIGN to inspire and provoke engagement, providing the reader with clear visual representations of each non-fiction topic.

AUTHOR INSIGHT:
CHARIS MATHER

Charis Mather is a children's author at BookLife Publishing who has a love for reading and writing. Her studies in linguistics and experiences working with young readers have given her a knack for writing material that suits a range of ages and skill levels. Charis is passionate about producing books that emphasise the fun in reading and is convinced that no matter how much you already know, there is always something new to learn.

PHASE 5
/er/

This book focuses on /er/ and the alternative pronunciations of its grapheme. It is a Purple level 8 book band.

Image Credits Images are courtesy of Shutterstock.com. With thanks to Getty Images, Thinkstock Photo and iStockphoto. Cover – Larina Marina, garetsworkshop, Oksana Chernenko, IgorMass. 3 – RagabGamal, Africa Studio, Prostock-studio, Monkey Business Images, Stokkete, SeventyFour 4–5 – Pixel-Shot, Dragon Images. 6–7 – Kues, BearFotos. 8–9 – MDV Edwards, Dreamer Company. 10–11 – ESB Professional, SpeedKingz. 12–13 – Phil Date, Dmytro Zinkevych. 14–15 – Andrii Medvednikov, MaKo-studio.

It is important that waiters note down orders perfectly. If a customer has a food allergy, getting the order mixed up could be very bad.

After waiters have taken people's orders, they transfer them to the chefs in the kitchen. While the customers wait for their food, waiters may offer them drinks.

Sometimes, customers may wave a waiter over to ask them for something. Waiters need to be alert for people who are trying to speak to them.

When the food is cooked, waiters bring it from the kitchen to the customers. A good waiter will remember which person ordered which dish.

Often, waiters may carry several plates in one go so that people get their food all at the same time. They have to take care not to drop them or get their fingers in the food.

When the main meal is done, waiters may check if people will be getting dessert as well. If so, they will take orders again.

If people do not want dessert, they may ask for the check. Waiters then take the payment. If they served the customers well, they may even get a tip.

A tip is extra payment just for the waiter to say thank you.

When the customers have left, the only thing that is left to do is clean up. Waiters clear plates away and wipe things down. Then, they set up for the next round of hungry customers.

The next time you go out to eat, look out for the waiters that help you. Be sure to thank them for serving you!

©2023 BookLife Publishing Ltd.
King's Lynn, Norfolk, PE30 4LS, UK

ISBN 978-1-80505-092-6

All rights reserved. Printed in China.
A catalogue record for this book is available from the British Library.

Waiters
Written by Charis Mather
Designed by Isabella Croker

FSC MIX
Paper from responsible sources
FSC® C113515

An Introduction to BookLife Readers...

Our Readers have been specifically created in line with the London Institute of Education's approach to book banding and are phonetically decodable and ordered to support each phase of the Letters and Sounds document.

Each book has been created to provide the best possible reading and learning experience. Our aim is to share our love of books with children, providing both emerging readers and prolific page-turners with beautiful books that are guaranteed to provoke interest and learning, regardless of ability.

BOOK BAND GRADED using the Institute of Education's approach to levelling.

PHONETICALLY DECODABLE supporting each phase of Letters and Sounds.

EXERCISES AND QUESTIONS to offer reinforcement and to ascertain comprehension.

CLEAR DESIGN to inspire and provoke engagement, providing the reader with clear visual representations of each non-fiction topic.

AUTHOR INSIGHT:
CHARIS MATHER

Charis Mather is a children's author at BookLife Publishing who has a love for reading and writing. Her studies in linguistics and experiences working with young readers have given her a knack for writing material that suits a range of ages and skill levels. Charis is passionate about producing books that emphasise the fun in reading and is convinced that no matter how much you already know, there is always something new to learn.

PHASE 5 /er/

This book focuses on /er/ and the alternative pronunciations of its grapheme. It is a Purple level 8 book band.

Image Credits Images are courtesy of Shutterstock.com. With thanks to Getty Images, Thinkstock Photo and iStockphoto. Cover – Larina Marina, garetsworkshop, Oksana Chernenko, IgorMass. 3 – RagabGamal, Africa Studio, Prostock-studio, Monkey Business Images, Stokkete, SeventyFour 4–5 – Pixel-Shot, Dragon Images. 6–7 – Kues, BearFotos. 8–9 – MDV Edwards, Dreamer Company. 10–11 – ESB Professional, SpeedKingz. 12–13 – Phil Date, Dmytro Zinkevych. 14–15 – Andrii Medvednikov, MaKo-studio.